SPEAKING SILENCE

Nazir Ahmed Shawl

AuthorHouse™ UK Ltd.
500 Avebury Boulevard
Central Milton Keynes, MK9 2BE
www.authorhouse.co.uk
Phone: 08001974150

© *2010 Nazir Ahmed Shawl. All rights reserved.*

No part of this book may be reproduced, stored in a retrieval system, or transmitted by any means without the written permission of the author.

First published by AuthorHouse 3/5/2010

ISBN: 978-1-4490-5670-4 (sc)

This book is printed on acid-free paper.

Dedication	vii
Contents	ix
An Introductory Word	xiii
Preface	xv
Author's Introduction	xvii

This book is dedicated to the Kashmiri people and their 'imprisoned paradise'

Contents

The Grace of Providence	1

Exhortations

A Clarion Call	3
Can we afford a Slip?	4
Conquering Evil	5
Estrangement	7
From Darkness to Light	8
Kashmir will Awaken the World	10
Line of Control	12
My Frozen Dream	14
No-One can bar My Way	15
Suicide	17
The Cherished Goal	18
The Glitter and the Goal	19

Footprints

Across the Oceans I love you more	22
A Pleasant Bite	23
Barak Obama	24
Benazir – A tribute	25
Eternal Memories of My Father.	27
Great People	29
Imam Hussain (ASW)	31
Mona Lisa – Incarnation	32
On Seeing a Portrait of my Brother	33

Quaid-i-Azam	34
Remembering Ali Kiani	35
Remembering Zulfiqar Ali Bhutto	37
The Bard of the East	39
The Death of Humanity	40

Nostalgia

Apharwat	43
Autumn in Kashmir	44
Hazratbal	45
Let the Flood of Hatred Subside	46
Nostalgia	47
Not Far Behind is the Spring Breeze	48
Resurrection	49
The Long Wait	50
Varamul	52
Wular Lake	53

Festivals

Barbeque	55
Hairath	56
Merry Christmas	57
My Eid Day	59
My Valentine	60
On Sighting the Eid Moon	61

Out of the Depths

A Priceless Thought	63
An Invitation	64
Do the Moments Die?	65
Infinity	66

Just in Sight	67
Lost Dream	68
Self-speaking	69
Solitude versus Fortitude	70
The Unsung Song	71
Unexpected Expectation	73
When Shall the Mercy Flow?	74

Love

Award	76
Eternal Love	77
Flashback	78
Morning Breeze	80
Peace	81
The Conquest	82
Unfinished Task	83

Reminiscences

A Father's Apology	85
Death of Dal Lake	87
Ecstasy	88
Immortal	89
Journey to the Unconscious	90
Paradise Turned into Hell	91
Repeat, Repeat!	92
The Flower Vale Cries Out for Spring	93
The Land of Gloom	95

Humanity

A Tribute to Londoners	97
Dreams Cannot be Sold	99

Echoes of Palestine	100
God's Handwriting	101
Long live Humanity	103
The Rest of the Windows are Shut	105
Will You Be My Friend?	106

My Country

A Perfect Dawn	109
Echoes of Kashmir	110
My Birthright	112
My Destiny	114
October 8th - Disaster in South Asia	116
Questions	117
Salvation	118
Simmering Disaster	119
The Phoenix of Kashmir	120

An Introductory Word

This collection of poems by a prominent member of the Kashmiri Diaspora is another testimony of the hold English easily acquires on the minds of people who do not own it as their mother tongue. They have willingly let it affect the shape of their thoughts, the accent of their feelings and the tone of their relationships. While British colonialism has passed into history and American hegemony faces recurrent challenge, English continues quietly to broaden its empire. This is not a result only of the global domination of the English-speaking peoples. It demonstrates the quality of the tongue. Supple in its nature, English has gained more plasticity by supplementing the means of expression of peoples of diverse temperaments and traditions.

However, what has occurred is not a one-way bargain. A cost is borne by the native English speaker. He has at least to tolerate, if not enjoy, ways of feeling and manners of speech, that if he were left alone, he would deem as at least uncongenial, if not awkward and strange.

Nazir Shawl's resort to English is of particular interest because the anguish and longing that permeate much of his work are more collective than purely personal. The currently prevailing Kashmiri consciousness gains a dual focus from the beauty of the land, on one side, and its desolation, on the other. The first – nature's gift – is condemned to be a passive witness to the second – the sedulous work of alien military occupation. A people who sustained a proudly independent existence for centuries and later basked in the Mughul empire, delighting in their arts and crafts, have had to suffer varied depredations at the hands of usurpers since the anarchic decline of that empire. These have reached a crescendo during the last sixty years. In the 1990's particularly, rapine and slaughter were visited on Kashmir which are unmatched in the chronicles of local tyranny and, indeed, were unimaginable before. Besides ravaging the population, the unreversed aggression has taken an untold psychic toll.

However, resilience is one of the glories of the human spirit, Kashmiri or otherwise. Nazir Shawl's poems are an example. He has not only suffered the tribulations of exile from his home. He has had to face the even more painful dispersal of the forces of liberation due in great part to the discouragement caused by the perverse policies of the world powers and their cynical disregard of the principles of freedom and peace they tirelessly proclaim. Yet he is certain that though the oppressor is triumphant and his victory is seemingly solid, it is hollow inside and will prove to be but a passing phase.

M. Yusuf Buch

Preface

You know what it is like to be walking down a street, or out in the countryside and suddenly a thought comes to consciousness – a thought that you did not know you were thinking – a thought which, by its sudden coming into being surprises you with its insolence, its tenacity and its faint, far distant echo of something overdue, perhaps profound – and you feel you must pay heed. It is like finding a shapeless pebble on the river bank or on some stony beach and you examine it wondering if inside some precious stone may lurk.

Shawl's poems bring to mind such things that in themselves, upon reflection with a little chipping and closer study, reveal gems like burning beacons that transmit light to each other and to the reader, with a glow that shines with tender warmth, addressing his longings, confiding his fears, his fantasies and his failures.

Each such discovered gem reveals an aspect of one man's progress through life; a glimpse into his soul; an empathy reaching out to share and to be shared by kindred spirits – by souls that too, are on a quest for something purer, the essence of which, though deeply embedded in the religious, political and ethnic troubles of Kashmir, Pakistan, India and the Middle East, is beyond time and place; belonging to the inner sanctuaries of the mind, the deeper recesses of the human spirit.

We feel, as we read, a sense which we share with Shawl, of judgement and of being judged. We want to turn aside but are held by a certain fascination that these thoughts are our own thoughts; these feelings are our own feelings, and we hear, through Shawl's individual medium of expression in a style and in a language that belies his mother tongue, cultural and ethnic background, a clear message, at times couched in subtle humour but, nevertheless, an urgent plea; the devout prayer of a sincere man on an earnest mission.

Adrian S Sherrard
Editor

Author's Introduction

"Speaking Silence" - a compilation of my poems is in your hands. It has been my endeavour to ensure that what I have written sees the light of day and confess that whatever I have intimately experienced I have tried to depict to the best of my knowledge and satisfaction. The reader will judge to what extent I may have succeeded in this venture.

This endeavour is fuelled by my yearnings, failures and successes, my hopes and dreams; it is about my nostalgia, my memories, sweet or sour. My mother, as well as my motherland, is reflected in my compositions. Contemporary events, which cast their shadow on our present-day history, have also been treated according to my understanding of them, as have persons and personalities who are revered by me – in recognition of their contribution to this work.

I belong to the disputed state of Jammu and Kashmir. The conflict here has ripped apart families and torn the social fabric to pieces and given birth to satanic human tragedy. Because of this, unfortunately, I was deprived in my childhood, of the academic guidance of my scholarly elder brother, Bashir Ahmed. After I left Kashmir I also lost my brother-in-law, Mir Ghulam Mohammad and his wife at Sopore for singing the freedom song. Both were victims of state violence.

This compilation of poems is the result of encouragement received from various well-wishers and friends from time to time:-

My father, the late Kh Noor-ud-Din Shawl always encouraged me to expand the horizons of my knowledge, virtually selecting reading materials for me in my school days; and my mother's sweet melodious rhymes lulled me to sleep into an appreciation of the power of music.

The late Professor Mohi-u-din Hajini, a great Kashmiri genius who showed appreciation for my early attempts at presenting papers, encouraged me in my literary pursuits as did Dr Agha Ashraf Ali, an outstanding Kashmiri intellectual who encouraged the development of my powers of debate and argument until he announced 'You have killed me with my own weapon', but insisting that you 'have the energy but no knowledge'- and proceeded forthwith to prepare a long list of books I was to read under the guidance and instruction of Professor Syed Habibullah, who was already a dear brother to me, and with whom I shared the enjoyment and appreciation of the poetry of Iqbal. I also shared with him his suffering and distress when a conspiracy was hatched to destroy him. Many never acknowledged his competence and creativity yet he was a great influence and a help in directing my quest for knowledge and wisdom.

My leaving Kashmir deprived me of the company of many valued friends and during my absence from Kashmir nobody looked after my family better than Kh Mehboob Ehali and his illustrious wife Mohtarma Salma Yasmeen Nagmi. I owe a debt of gratitude also to the 'Iffat' Urdu magazine, for affording me thought-provoking editorials and wonderful articles that have stimulated my thinking and influenced my attitudes.

Dr. Khalid Jehangir Qazi, would always enquire about my latest poems and take a few back with him to Buffalo USA for publication, whenever he visited London.

Among the many well-wishers to be acknowledged is Ershad Malik who goaded me into publishing this work, also the tireless supporter of my efforts, the author of 'Punchline in Greater Kashmir', GM Zahid. To him, and to the large number of friends and acquaintances who repeatedly sent me mail in appreciation of those poems, which were published at various times in different newspapers around the world, I am grateful.

I owe a deep debt of gratitude to Ambassador Mohammad Yusuf Buch, a Kashmiri living in exile, a former journalist and diplomat having served as a special adviser to the Secretary General of the United Nations, is a great source of inspiration to me and has kindly consented to write a foreword to the present work.

My patient and untiring editor Adrian Sherrard has given his precious time through the long winter nights editing this work and I am indeed both fortunate to have discovered him and deeply grateful. I also thank his wife Madame Chiu Ik Sing who played a generous hostess during my frequent sessions to their home with her charm and wonderful hospitality.

My three children, Mansoor, Yasir and Sobia were always the first to know about my latest creations and it was their tears which brought me to understand the strength of feeling and the sense of loss incurred of loved ones who had disappeared into the realm of the unknown, and to whom tribute is duly paid in my poems. Mansoor's wife, Maria, is a new arrival in our family and she also shares our love of literary pursuits.

Never last and never least is Shamim, my life's partner, who always appreciated my poetic sensitivities and has been a tireless support in my earnest desire to reach out, to communicate my feelings to readers and to her is my deepest regard for that constant support.

Nazir Ahmed Shawl
August 2009

The Grace of Providence
'Long Cosmic Night'

In the sunshine of a futuristic vision,
As a basis for humanity's cohesion
He changes the course of a storm,
Undaunted, unmoved by any harm.
He continues treading His straight path
Unmindful of the intensity of oceanic wrath.

He is all that is human when speaking of gain;
Come to this planet to give balm and unchain.
Those fettered and freed kiss the dust of His feet
To watch Him go by, is a blessed treat.

He controls the breaths of revolutionary gales
The vast caravan of humanity is tied to His sails.
He conquers all space; guides the River of Time,
The galaxies wait to be blessed in their prime.

His turban reflects all the great dazzling Light,
In the clumps of the stars in the long cosmic night
Spread in the heavens like profuse green grass.
Listen, and to His chain in your hand hold fast.

For His voice is in water, in air and in sand
That He showers all blessings on every land,
There is ample evidence
He, by His most magnanimous grace,
Is Providence.

Exhortations

Your chains clank with freedom cries
Rebellion thunders; tyranny defies

Nazrul-Islam "Awake"

A Clarion Call
Can We Afford a Slip?
Conquering Evil
Estrangement
From Darkness to Light
Kashmir Will Awaken the World
Line of Control
My Frozen Dream
No One Can Bar my Way
Suicide
The Cherished Goal
The Glitter and the Goal

A Clarion Call

I became a nomad for the sake of my land
Freedom is my cry I drum my band.
The people of my land are on my side
My occupier friends are savage and wild.
I am dreaming my dream with all the chill,
My tormentors are practising their shoot-to-kill.

I heeded the call and marched on the road;
Left my little kingdom to sail on the board,
- A wingless bird craving a nest -
My creed is noble and I'll try my best.
Prison, torture and exile deter not my bet,
Wherever I am I will fume and fret.

Do not indict me; what is my crime?
The cuckoo tells me 'Your goal is sublime'.
Extinguish the fires and wait for the song,
All woes will melt - the journey is long.
Evoke not my anger; I have burnt my boats,
Stop teasing my people - do not cut their throats.

The breeze of freedom will blow very fast
Unite all your ranks and bury your past.

This poem describes the collective pain of Kashmir

Can we afford a Slip?

All over the globe strange winds blow,
Surprisèd wise-men beat their brow.
In the vastness of the skies dark clouds flow,
The horrible lightening makes a terrible show.

The atmosphere seems drowned in gloom,
Moving around are angels of doom.
Pain has flooded every hut and home,
For wandering in the wilderness there is no room.

Brave men always brave the storms,
For the good of a nation they open their arms.
They author a future by breaking all norms.
They are all assets, the promising charms.

Gather the courage, put the nation on the rails,
Do not be obsessed with ignominious tales.
Shake off the lethargy and tighten your sails,
You have to overcome all storms and gales.

All hatreds be conquered.
Come captain your ship!
Stand up and be counted!
We can't have a slip
'Twixt cup and lip.

Conquering Evil

Enemies of peace are firing shots,
Blowing up other people's plots,
The saner voices do surmise,
It is a matter of great surprise.
Blood spills like torrential rain,
Who opiated those human wills?
Life all over is in great disdain,
Who is behind the blast that kills?
Should we from such acts refrain?
Everywhere there is agony and pain.

But sanity has a demanding role,
Bring humanity to its cherished goal.
End starvation; end the hunger,
Educate people to make them stronger,
Religions preaching peace and harmony,
Should shun every form of wretched acrimony.

End exploitation; end the bias,
Try to become humanely pious,
Raise the banner of justice and peace,
'There is no justice without truth,
There is no truth without peace,
There is no peace without justice.'
Raise the banner against zealots,
Shun the criminals and shun the despots,
Feel the pain and feel the chill,
Respect the other person's will.

Let's not lose hope,
There is great scope,
The reckoning word is 'unity'.
For the greater good of humanity,
Untie the knots of your mind,
Love others and be kind,

By abhorring acrimony of all sorts
Terminate the canker of terrorist plots.

We understand the gravity of the situation,
Against such depravity this is our determination:
By commitment, dedication,
And foresight.
To end the feuding and the fight.

This message to the estrangèd few:-
"Polish up your thoughts,
Open up your hearts,
Come back and live as humans do.
Identify the causes and the source,
This'll bless your future's course."

Then, as one, we all shall proudly say
We have conquered the evil day.

Estrangement

Slavery is a philosophy.
Cowardice is nurtured by thoughtless apathy.
Fear is a feeling
Ingrained in the fire of fearful beauty.

The voice of conscience sold,
Overlaps the wisdom of Plato,
The upright truthfulness of Socrates,
And the encyclopaedic comprehension of Aristotle,
Manifold.

The brave and courageous
Move ahead undaunted.
Through forests of clouds thick and dense,
They conquer the borders of common sense,
Create in themselves, at last, a defence
Of injustice, exploitation, the targeted offence.

They expect men of conscience thereby will be roused.
There'll be no more grouses.
All quarrels will be doused.

However, there is much concern in the mind
For morals and values that have so declined
Of the prayer leaders in the prayer halls
Being replaced by robots.
Such preachers will learn blindly to recite
Like parrots
The words of the chief -
Though he's often not right
And a proven thief.

From antiquity they will receive punishment,
Let us rise to reverse this estrangement.

From Darkness to Light

Today I am reminded of the darkest night
No moon, no stars, no ray of light.
The terrible silence the painful sight
Life was hanging in the grimmest plight.

Two leading minds were making pledges
They were walking on knife-edges,
With determination stark and grim
They kept their word through thick and thin.

That night shivered young and old
This very thought makes me feel cold.
My love of truth was making me sigh
This was a matter of do *and* die.

Restraints all vanished, there was no score
It led to an unending war.
Liberation was the aim and creed
Let all of us come in on this deed.

To overcome shades of darkest night
Move on to kindle the shining light.
Rise and conquer fear and fright
Distinguish between wrong and right.

End the feuds, end the fight
Make the world a little bright.
Humanity needs a ray of light
People of the world unite.

We must engage one and all
We must give a clarion call.
Nobody is too short or tall
No one is too big or small.

Thinking upsets the old power game
Is this not a crying shame?

Respecting others is a wondrous tool
Let us follow this golden rule.
Let us oust all hateful thoughts
Let us share the love of sports!
Let us follow a rule of sorts.

Hatred and plotting we will defeat.
The *dénouement* we will soon complete
Good days will come by change of mind.
Inspiration will make you kind.

'Might is right' is a thesis old
Conquer *the hearts* of young and old!

Kashmir will Awaken the World

I know you and your woes and wails
A timekeeper is recording your sad tales.
News from your place is usually bad.
To hear of such suffering makes us sad.

Lunging from crises into catastrophe
The tongue loses power to express and to speak of it.
The question I put to the world keepers of peace is this:-
'When shall this ill-wind of repression cease?'

Murder, genocide, coercion and terror -
People disappearing in this period of horror.
Every village and town is in a complete shambles,
Even the tormentor is irked by their scrambles.

Dreams continue to cloud my eyes,
My finer feelings are steeped in my sighs
I cry out to Thee at the genocide -
Oh Lord give ear to my woeful cries.

Contractors of conscience have retreated in deep jungles,
The sources of their light hid in crevices and bangles.
The leaves of the plane trees have seriously caught fire,
Just staying alive has become dare and dire.

Those of conviction carry their cross.
The nightingale searches alas, at her loss,
All over, a silence has descended in gloom
The conscience-sellers with swords and guns roam.

This history's in the making -
Blood of the dearest it's staking.
My fellow countrymen listen, rejoice!
My ears are ringing with Mahjoor's strong voice:

"The time will come when the world we shall rouse.
Kashmiris sing out this song and be proud!"

Mahjoor is Kashmir's national poet

Line of Control
- adapted from Kashmiri -

From across the mountains very high,
My homeland beckoned with a sigh.
The scented winds sang melodious songs,
Undaunted, I journeyed to correct the wrongs.

I was stopped and turned back:
"You cannot proceed along this track.
Show the permit to go ahead,
Not an inch further may you tread."
The patriot in me then came out:
I thundered with a mighty shout,
"I am the heir of all this land,
I am from this paradise grand.
My mother on the other side let me trace.
'Tis her homeland, her birth place!
The winds from that dear side of strife
Sounded for me the message of life."

I was stopped, but
My head was not chopped.
I was dubbed lunatic and mad.
This behaviour made me sad.
I was taunted and ridiculed,
But refused to be dictated to and ruled.

Between me and my mother
Over the years has come a wall,
I can do no other
To bring about its fall.
Many an innocent life,
Bruised by bayonet and knife.
Such rude shock and violent expression
Enough to cause sorrow and deep depression

In a person abhorring such vile repression.
My altercation was in vain,
With rulers or leaders it was the same.
None of them could I compel,
Neither could I cast the spell.
I moved towards the border wall.
The moustached man gave me a call.

I fell down. I bled.

A bird flew free, far over my head.
He cheered and clapped his wings,
Over my laughing wounds he sings!

I ask myself the question,
Am I the crown of creation?

The **Line of Control** is Kashmir's 'Berlin Wall'

My Frozen Dream

A whiff of the morning breeze
Came my way, hit me, to tease
The soft touch of this pure air,
Arousing me for something rare.

It gave life to some of my dreams
Which wandered, tuned to the musical streams.
I became free of strife
Got a new lease of life.

The night descended with the birth of the moon
Which started gazing at me soon.
And I drowned in the waves of the moonlit night
Intoxicated in pure delight.

I forgot every pain
I broke every chain.
I gave wheels to my wings
I unhitched all my strings.

Suddenly a tsunami of emotions was unfurled,
For me it was a completely different world.
Hypocrisy, double standards and the lies
Carried me away from my murmurings and sighs.

I swam with an over-burdened lot
To scupper and defeat every scheming plot.
I am standing firm on my own home ground;
And still can hear a melodious sound.

My people await, with anxiety, my return
They want to meet and greet me turn by turn.
Voracious creatures will meet their end,
All the usurpers will have to bend,
Concede to me my birthright
And call off their greedy fight.

No-One can bar My Way

With no axe to grind
I made up my mind
To face the storms
Forsake the norms
Side with the oppressed
Fight the oppressor
Raise my voice
Respect individual's choice.
In vales and peaks
Stop the shrieks
Keep the tormentors at bay -
No one can bar my way.

Mirror the people's dreams,
Scatter the dazzling beams,
Light the lamps of hope,
Untie the knotted rope.
Help the weak and old
Weigh them with silver and gold.
For ending miseries untold
Make them strong and bold.
Conquer the minds to say -
No one can bar my way.

People are not small fry
Do not feed them a lie;
They have force and might
They have every right.
Let them sing their songs
To undo the wrongs
To stake their claims
To attain their aims.
I have a hope today -
No one can bar my way.

We have taken a step
We will keep it up
In darkness or light
The target's in sight.

With courage we'll talk
We'll continue to walk
Leaving unturned no stone

Each obstacle, boulder or rock
With courage we will knock.
In ocean and river
The enemy will quiver.
And, at the end of the day -
No one shall bar our way.

Our limit is not just the sky
We have to soar very high
Where eagles echo this cry -
'Up to the stars you fly.
Do not heave a sigh
Again and again you try.'
Greatness at our feet will lie.
All evils we have to foil
We, the true sons of the soil,
With courage we state:
"Our Allah is great!"

My dream will come true, one day -
No-one can bar my way.

Suicide

All dreams remain shattered;
All alphabets scattered,
Their letters join to become words
And these become sharp-edged swords,
A challenge for all selfish despots,
A warning for unbridled zealots:
These feuds and self-ignited strife
Universally threaten all human life.

Words can be a soothing balm,
Soothing emotions, in a world of charm.
For every Harry, Tom, Dick or Shawn
Great words of wisdom can still this storm.

Bring sense to the mad mobs of thugs in Gujarat
For the victims of the frenzy, trembles my heart.
Implore Sharon, end the siege of Yasser Arafat,
Bring a fragrant new dawn to Harwan and Nishat.

Call on world powers to attend to this plight,
Be not hoodwinked by the oppressor's might
Invoke the world echelons, unshackle their voice,
Forbid the oppressor to ransack and rejoice.

The fate of the hapless is ever the same.
For all of mankind – a terrible shame.
Oppression of all kinds must surely now cease,
We must all co-exist in tranquility and peace.

Visionaries of power - come forward and guide!
Or else, all my words, will commit suicide.

Harwan and **Nishat** are Mughul gardens on the banks of the Dal Lake in Kashmir
Harwan is now a National Park

The Cherished Goal

Asking to be directed and alerted.
A lost traveller in a desert, deserted,
I carry in my bosom the thorns of life,
Unending pain, and misery and strife.

A well thought out title I have to find,
An unwritten tale fermenting in the mind,
The desert's barrenness spells a day of doom,
A hell of a commotion and a well of gloom.

The war of identity confronts my dreams,
The cycle of chaos is teasing my heart,
The times are also testing my means.
The stormy winds and the sand smart.

No sandstorm can impede my way,
My strength is my unfettered grace.
Raise your hands for me and pray.
All my people in my arms enlace.

Let us purify our mind and soul
Attain together our cherished goal.

The Glitter and the Goal

On all paths and subways are scattered the thorns,
And ferocious animals with outrageous horns.
The reason, the logic and immortal rationale
Swept away by a storm, irrational, banal
The opera, the theatre the dazzling band
Just a castle erected on slippery sand.

Speed in a journey usually thrills
But a crazy leap most often kills.
In many a book as I have read,
Shakespeare has rightly said
'All that glisters is not gold
Fare you well, your suit is cold'.
The musical tunes of chatter-box
Was a calculated illusion or a hoax?
I voluntarily entered the booby trap
Which turned out to be a bloody mishap.

The dreams are gone with the horrifying night
Realities that confront me in a mesmerising sight.
What unforeseen, mysterious, wicked human strife!
I bleed from the wounds inflicted with my own knife.
Repentance, weeping, wailing and the shedding of tears
Has had the effect of only strengthening all of my fears.
My projected approximations were so far from my will,
Pain has quickly overtaken the incipient and latent chill.
Come out and abandon this horrendous, this fetid state.
Do not become entangled in a prolonged, futile debate.
Have trust in the ultimate, the final, divine reality.
Trust God's power - His absolute sovereignty.

Shun all the prophets and preachers of doom.
Abandon all forms of madness and gloom
Do not stagnate, stand up and move!
To all the people you have to prove

We face every challenge with pride.
The power of our goal's on our side.
The distractions and impediments
　Will all be made to withdraw
　And all the haughty culprits
　Will bow down to the floor.

Footprints

On the dry desert dunes
I looked for your footprints

Salik Popatia "I knew not"

Across the Oceans I Love You More
A Pleasant Bite
Barak Obama
Benazir – A Tribute
Eternal Memories of My Father
Great People
Imam Hussain
Mona Lisa
On Seeing a Portrait of My Brother
Quaid-i-Azam
Remembering Ali Kiani
Remembering Zulfiqar Ali Bhutto
Bard of the East
The Death of Humanity

Across the Oceans I love you more
- *Remembering Dr Agha Ashraf Ali* -

I am reminded of your poetic prose,
Radiating thoughts and the fragrant rose.
It has kindled in me a ray of light,
The desire to grasp and further the fight.

In an unlimited ocean dark
You were a solitary shining spark.
I will always carry this thought with pride
That you helped to inspire my creative side.

In helping, you respected my self-esteem
To realise in me my most-prized dream.
You stand now before me in your grace
Looking straight into my eyes and face.

Telling me to 'know thyself'
By reading books from every shelf.
My encounter with the great debate
Has opened wide the literary gate.

People here just dance and date
While I write up my precious fate.
One day we'll reach the far-off shore
Across the oceans I love you more.

Dr Agha Ashraf Ali has been my guide in my journey of self-discovery

A Pleasant Bite

As lightening strikes when clouds collide
And the air is filled with the crash of thunder,
I'm carried away on a great rip tide
With pangs of pain, my heart asunder
To some far-off raging, roaring shore.

It's then I forget all my wrangles
Hear your mesmerising poetry
Your musical lore
See your colourful bangles
Your radiant face, a symbol of pride,
A rosy fragrance danced with the bride.
They cannot quench their spiritual thirst
Who drink unlimited cups and do not burst.

In my wine-drenched fantasies in the public square
Fiddling and fondling your fragrant hair,
You snatched my glass, declared a war!
And wine drops fell on every star.

You poured on me a spiritual grace,
You rightly put me in my place,
The memory I can never efface.

Do not punish me for all my wrongs,
In the gardens of London I hear your songs.
In the silent moments of a moonlit night
The bittersweet memory is a pleasant bite.

Barak Obama
America's latest face

African Americans have a moment of pride
The people's power is on their side,
The spirit of 'King' has realised a dream.
Equality flowers your self esteem
Blacks are writing their desired fate
They've conquered the olden syndrome of hate.

Obama has gotten his prized gift
It is a milestone, a wondrous shift.
All Americans now are dancing with joy
Every Man and woman, girl and boy.

Conflicts, tensions, recession and war;
Humanity at large bears this burden sore:
Obama inherits the legacy of Bush,
To jump out of the cauldron he needed no push.

Across the oceans we should hear this song:
'Hatred will vanish; the road is long'.
The ascending road is very steep
The custodians of peace have been asleep.

Obama, please honour Kashmir's aspired goal
Put balm on our bruises and play your role.
The White House greets you in all good grace;
High up on Mt. Rushmore we'll see your face!

Benazir – A tribute

In atmosphere ceremonial
Chanting of slogans most jovial
People gyrating with joy and goodwill
The throng of the occasion a magnificent thrill;
An ocean of folk at the peak of emotion.
An unprecedented act of devotion.

As the leader emerged from the car to wave hands
Time froze and fell silent all drums and all bands
All of a sudden all was in shock
Nobody moved. Everything stopped.

The environs too were frozen in time;
Clouds on the horizon stopped in a line.
Shrieks and wails then came from yonder,
Every eye began then to wander.

I would have to say, in brief,
Every soul was stricken with grief.
Blood was flowing,
Whistles blowing
Voices wailing
Eyes a-weeping
Hearts a-bleeding
Thoughts condemning.

Someone very dear,
A leader and a seer,
Dynamic, very great,
Assassinated for a trait.

Called 'The daughter of the East',
She fell to the frenzy of a beast.
She had rekindled a gleam of hope
When she walked the high tightrope.

Benazir longed for a new day to dawn.
She stood for a stable and strong Pakistan.
But although Benazir was so great and nice
She gambled and cast the political dice;
Undaunted, she paid the ultimate price.

Eternal Memories of My Father.

In a wilderness on some foreign strand
On my own two feet again I stand.
I remember with love my land of birth
It always fills me with joy and mirth.

Some time back on an ocean shore
My wounds blossomed in a bleeding sore
And I found myself in solitude
But I soon fought back with fortitude.

In my loneliness I turned a page
And on it found a pictured sage.
He has ever been so dear
For me he has shown loving care.

He took me out to hills and vales
Where he told me most delightful tales.
He gave meaning to my screaming;
He guided me in all my dreaming.

All his friends owe him this debt;
He cared for all with great respect.
Living with him has been a dream,
Embodiment of true self-esteem.

Only friends had he, no foes.
He shared in everybody's woes.
He, majestic, sweet and tall,
Bore the name Noor-Uddin Shawl.

The last I saw him was at Lahore.
I kissed his feet in terrified lore.
Whims and fancies racked my brain
When he boarded the Samjota train.

All my children cried in pain
Their tears were mingling with the rain.
Although I lost all physical contact
His brimming love stayed always intact.

One fine evening on the phone
I heard in very gloomy tone;
Moments vanished thick and fast
Finally he had breathed his last.

Whenever I hear a soothing sound
A thousand memories dance around.
I feel his warmth e'en here, today
For me he is a glistening ray.

In good deeds done he was so keen;
His life was gracious and serene.
He was God's blessing and a light
He stood for freedom, justice, right!

Seeing him speak was a bracing sight.
His words were stunning, lucid, bright.
So far from Varamul, mountain, hill,
These memories bring me solace still.

I miss my father every day more.
His absence is a permanent sore.

The Samjota train is the one linking India with Pakistan
This poem was composed on Brighton beach in the United Kingdom

Great People

On the 12th of February a tragedy struck
Indian forces ran amuck.
It was a freezing winter's day
All the people were kept at bay.
Troops were armed from head to toe,
The seeds of fear they had to sow.
There was a lot of terror, gloom and chill
Troops went out to shoot and kill.
People were gathered in a ground
Many a rumour spread around.
Suddenly the troops went on the rampage,
For India they wrote a dreadful page.
Weak people die a stray dog's death
Brave people do not stop to count their breath.
In death they live throughout all time;
People sing their lore,
With rhythm and with rhyme.

A chapter of timidity wrote a man,
He feared the prison and the chain.
He bargained for his life in pain
For the sake of his children and his wife.
For the troops he became a guide;
He took the troops to the hide.
There, hid a warrior with his guard;
Arrested by deceit and fraud.
Troops had fixed a price on his head
They wanted him alive or dead.
Taken to the college ground
Locals heard his fatal sound.
Shot for his creed
A glorious deed.
Shot too, was his wife,
They took her life.
It pains my every thought.

I shall remember the two with pride
This, my children shall be taught;
Don't cast the thought aside,
Remember them both forevermore
Such great people turn the tide.

The incident happened in 1995 in the town of Sopore in Kashmir, when my brother-in-law and his wife were killed.

Imam Hussain (ASW)

Hussain epitomizes a righteous creed
He did not submit to the dictates of Yazeed.
He responded to a historic need
He performed a matchless, glorious deed.

With his sacred blood a great chapter he wrote
With great pride this supreme act we quote.
He will live till sun, moon and stars cease to shine
He represents my ideal, exquisite and fine.

Yazeed symbolises evil and strife
Hussain attained eternal life.
Hussain is the determination of Lion of God (RA)
He remained steadfastly true to Allah's nod.

The earth of Karbala is sacred and red
Where the blood of the greatest martyr was shed.
The Prophet's (SAW) most dear was brave, noble and bold,
His companions as well suffered miseries untold.

Karbala for all virtuous people is Light,
For conquering evil we must ceaselessly fight.
Hussain's grandeur always lives in my heart
His grand sacrifice enlightens my thought.

Yazeed was condemned for his untimely deed,
To follow Hussain is a timely need.

Imam Hussain was beheaded at **Karbala**, a city in Iraq, in 680 AD. (See 'Remembering Zulfiqar Ali Bhutto')
ASW – 'May Allah's blessing be upon him'
SAW – 'May Allah's peace and blessings be upon him' this is said whenever the name of the prophet Muhammad is mentioned or read (in Arabic)
RA – Means 'May Allah be pleased with him'

Mona Lisa – Incarnation

Always when for work I leave,
The wayward winds make me believe
Nature's bounties you must perceive,
Priceless ideas you can conceive.

It was a glazing day.
Sun was shining in the brightest way,
I alighted on a bus in haste
No single moment could I waste.
I arrived at Stratford for my train,
Lots of ideas stormed in my brain.
Soon I rushed to cover some ground,
By God's grace the train I found.
Inside, it dawned there was no seat.
Standing with ease was also a treat.

Somebody knocked strongly at my mind,
A prolonged glance appeared warm and kind;
Before me stood Leonardo's art
So elegant, amazing, tender, smart,
On each side of her face, hair cascaded, rolled,
An in-depth, well-meaning un-told story, told.
Ocean-like eyes were very deep,
For long, it seemed they'd yearned to sleep.

Antiquity with me, now broke all ties -
Incarnated Mona Lisa was before my very eyes!

Stratford is part of Greater London

On Seeing a Portrait of my Brother

Pencil drawn lines had created the image;
It took me back the good times to envisage.
The dance of the memories took on a new shape
A tempest of music got switched on the tape.
My brother was there in all of his charm;
He stood there before me serene and calm.

He had his beliefs and unflinching creeds
Loved by all for his loving deeds.
He bowed to none but Allah almighty
He was thus ennobled by his Prophet's piety.
My brother was a source of the greatest pleasure
Full of love bestowed in plentiful measure.

Humility and greatness stood at his gate.
With hard work and devotion he followed his fate.
Before parting this world for his heavenly abode
On the highest pedestals of life he rode.
He never misused his authority or power
Maintaining his cool in his golden hour.

With affection he remembered the land of his birth,
Of such happy thoughts there was never a dearth.
He is always adored in my heart and my eyes,
He's forever alive in my thoughts and my sighs.
Magnanimity was cause of the fame that he had,
The name that he bore was Bashir Ahmad.

The last time I saw my brother was in 1987. He died in 1992

Quaid-i-Azam

He came as a towering inferno,
A messiah,
To light the lamps of hope
Instil confidence and conquer fear,
To resist exploitation and subjugation.
He became the darling of the masses,
A father of the nation.
The tallest of the tall
For one and for all.
Responding to his nation's call
With an articulate voice
He cast his dice
And kept on walking the formidable road
With vision and his dream.
Like a vessel and anchor,
The captain of a ship,
With a glowing lamp
Conquering the darkness
And opening the paths to the doors of dawn,
Which brought into existence
A new homeland,
Pakistan.
All exclaimed
Muhammad Ali Jinnah is a gem,
His people call him
Quaid-i-Azam.

Quaid-i-Azam is the title bestowed upon a supreme leader by Indian Muslims and was given to Muhammad Ali Jinnah, the founder of Pakistan

Remembering Ali Kiani

With a lot of memories in my head
I picked out a delicate thread.
I left for Sanctuary Street
Friends at the 'Jang' I had to meet.

I soon reached the second floor
And as I opened the office door
Fondest memories danced around
But I failed to hear the familiar sound.

When I glanced at the chair of my friend
The silence spoke.
All of us count our breath
And live in hope.
Last phase of life is death;
He had met his end.

He no more walked his favourite road
He'd left, instead, for his heavenly abode.
A truly professional sort,
Honest, forthright in every thought.

View his photo in the file
And you will see his charming smile.
He strove and proved himself quite clever
Portraying pain and man's endeavour.

With his pen he was quite fair;
He thought beyond his clan and race.
His trait of excellence we should share;
To his profession he brought grace.

He will live on, in my heart
With cherished memories, for my part.
I'll never forget the seat of his fame.
Ali Kiani was his name.

Ali Kiani was a journalist friend who died in 2008
The Jang is an Urdu newspaper published in London

Remembering Zulfiqar Ali Bhutto

Custodians of our justice,
Custodians of our State,
Hanged on the cross of connivance,
An adversary wise and great,
An outstanding genius
Who struggled against injustice,
Dreaming a myriad dreams not only for his people
But for all those oppressed in the world.
A charming orator, a towering person,
A restless but warm soul
Representing his people's aspiration
Earning their admiration
And treasured in their eyes.
He was a luminary, just and true.
By his murder justice, too,
Was hanged –
Thus rewriting a modern Karbala
And reviving the tradition of *Imam*
For his conviction and his righteousness.
History is a testimony providing a rightful place
To Bhutto, who was brave and bold,
Suffered miseries untold
For his beliefs at home and abroad
Authoring in a glorious page
By facing innumerable odds
Under the shadow of guns
And in the jaws of death.
He lives in every breath
In his people's consciousness.
He challenged the dancers of destruction
With his unfettered determination
Till he paid the price.
In the dark hour of that day

Death was trembling to say –
"What a great reward; how great an end!"
Then in the purity of the gallows wept and roared -
"Zulfiqar Ali Bhutto is living, not dead!"

Zulfiqar Ali Bhutto was hanged on the 4th April, 1979, in Central Jail, Rawalpindi in Pakistan
The Imam tradition refers to Imam Hussain, who was beheaded at **Karbala**, a city in Iraq, in 680 AD

The Bard of the East

Dr Iqbal, 'Bard of the East',
His poetry, an intellectual feast.
His imagination soars alarmingly high;
He delves deep down with an in-looking eye,
Portraying much suffering, sadness and pain.
Displaying a truly great and gifted brain.

He believed in the virtue of self-affirmation,
He opposed every concept of self-denigration.
His ideas revolved all around this same theme –
That humans should always have full self-esteem.
He advocated the eradication in one's own self
The pursuit of all pleasure, all power and all pelf.

To him life's a book to be read page by page;
This excellent devotion will make you a sage.
He prayed for commotion, calamity and storm
To ensure a new world of orderly form.
Ad aethera tendens' was his battle cry;
'Where eagles dare you try to fly'.

Till death comes, the weak die many times in great pain.
Self-reliance is needed for your strength to gain.
At Allahabad he announced this inner refrain.
Quaid was the architect, Iqbal the brain.

Ad aethera tendens' is the motto of SP College in Srinagar, meaning 'Reach for the sky'
Allahabad is the city in India where Nehru was born

The Death of Humanity
- A tribute to Daniel Pearl-

Daniel's death was a gruesome crime,
O righteous people it's a testing time.
Chopping off a head for its creations
Breeds hatred in different situations.
Condemn it with one voice
There is no other choice.

Great people perform great deeds,
Striving hard for their cherished creeds
They offer their blood for sacred needs,
Their precepts flourish and nourish these seeds.

Socrates loved the vision of truth,
The path he trod was far from smooth;
He drank the cup for truth's sake,
The vile poison his thirst did slake.

Who was Pearl? I do not know,
But my respect I'd like to show.
I too grieve with Pearl's wife,
She lost the partner of her life.

I, too, feel this sting of pain and profanity,
It makes me scorn this crass insanity.
My heart goes out to the journalist fraternity,
I join them in mourning this crime against humanity.
We have now one fewer in our writer's domain,
All are bound together as a human chain.
Let the people of the world arise,
Declare all mankind as equal and wise.

Dismantle greed and hostile occupation,
Strive to free every soul from alien domination.

Dan will live on in our hearts and minds,
For his daring deeds on behalf of mankind.

Let us pay him a deservéd tribute,
Let us end strife and every díspute,
Respect all people's wishes, and try
Not to treat them as small fry.
Let's salute Daniel's individuality,
His death is the death of all humanity.

Daniel Pearl - the Wall Street journalist beheaded in Karachi, Pakistan by terrorists

Loneliness

Whenever I am all alone
I clearly hear a ringing tone
To my understanding it is known
Around me many a jewel and precious stone

Nostalgia

Apharwat
Autumn in Kashmir
Hazratbal
Let the Flood of Hatred Subside
Nostalgia
Not Far Behind is the Spring Breeze
Resurrection
The Long Wait
Varamul
Wular Lake

Apharwat

Climbing the different mountain peaks
Refreshes eyes and brightens cheeks.
In warm, still air or gales and chill
It gives the hiker quite a thrill.

At times it creates a shiver in the spine
At times it lulls you in a realm sublime.
Away from work and office files
I footed a trek of seventy miles.
From Varamul up to Apharwat summit,
It was a joyful, wondrous fillip
Wearing a simple tee-shirt and jeans
I carried a stick and a bag of beans.

Alpathar Lake was on the way,
It looked like a shining silver tray.
Wani, Mir, Singh, Bijvoet and Borst,
They shared with me this joyous past.
I yearn still for that heavenly bliss,
It was a charming nature-kiss.
Go to the hills for wealth and fame -
It is a most enthralling game!

Apharwat is a peak in the Himalayas
Wani, Mir, Singh, Bijvoet and **Borst** were colleagues at St. Joseph's in Barramulla in 1971
Varamul is the Kashmiri name for the town of Barramulla

Autumn in Kashmir

After summer's dust and heat
The change to autumn is pleasant and sweet;
There's noise in the cornfields,
Farmers are harvesting their yields,
Hustle and bustle is in the courtyard,
Fruits arriving from every orchard.

In the market abundant fruits on sale
In hues of red, green, and pale.
Small village girls with their riches and rags
Collect fallen leaves to fill up their bags.
A housewife sits, knits or weaves
While her daughter chars the dried-up leaves.

On the roads move trucks, buses and cars
'Neath beautiful, majestic, gigantic chinars.
In summer these trees provide cooling shade;
In autumn their greenness will gradually fade
Soon their leaves become golden bright;
A most absorbing and wonderful sight.
Finally the leaves turn bright, burning red;
Today my imaginings picked up that thread.

Chinars have both - dark shade and bright fire.
Like my prized obsession - both dear and dire!

Chinar is a Persian word loosely meaning 'What fire!' – after the appearance of the autumnal reds of the leaves of the Chinar trees

Hazratbal

Exquisite, the shrine at Hazratbal
Serene on the banks of the charming Dal.
Its glistening stone in marble white
To be seen, is a truly wondrous sight.
Around it, is an aura of fragrant air,
Which adorns our Prophet's sacred hair.

Set in surroundings very fine
It glistens with grandeur in sunshine.
Although it has weathered many a storm
Yet still it keeps its attractive form.
Even during the darkest night
Its domes still shine and sparkle bright.

Pilgrims come visiting from early dawn.
It has a spacious garden and well-kept lawn
Where families picnic and lovers fawn.
In the evening they watch the sun's dying rays.
My *alma mater* urged my return
Thus, I remember the good, olden days.

Hazratbal is a shrine in Srinagar visited by thousands of pilgrims as it contains the sacred relic of a hair from the Prophet Mohammad (PBUH)

Let the Flood of Hatred Subside

The longing and loneliness I lull in my heart
In the dark of the night, awakens my thought.

Preoccupations knock hard at my mind.
Present with past, both together they bind.

Emerging from mist, Shawl, as a child,
The passionate, sensitive, meek and mild,

Surrounded by all the souls of great friends,
Revolving in galaxy of diamonds and gems.

They all stood by me, by sun and by shade,
Heartwarming, extravagant love they gave.

It is with my dear ones I long to abide.
Let love and humanity fill up that void.

The flood of all hatred, let it subside.

Nostalgia

I vividly remember my morning shuttle
 - As if I'd had to run for a battle.
I used to travel with my friends and foes
I shared with them my dreams and woes.

My mind still carries that pleasant load,
My friend dwelt near the Narabal road,
 Where the famous poplars grow -
 On each side of the road in rows.
In spring they are all green and white,
In autumn they become yellow and bright.

My duty called me, come rain or shine.
I honestly deployed my skills and time.
Sometimes I boarded for Char Chinar,
 Sometimes I dashed to Shalimar.

The music of fountains murmured around
 On Magalla Hill I heard that sound.
 When such moments come to mind
The forlorn present with the past I bind.

The poem was written in the foothills of the Sino-Himalayas, on **Magalla Hill** in the Punjab
Char Chinar is a small natural island in the Dal Lake with four Chinar trees, one on each of the four corners of the island
Shalimar is a Royal Mughul garden found along the banks of the Dal Lake

Not Far Behind is the Spring Breeze

My burden of memories I should unfold:
Kashmir's winter is very cold.
Kangri, Pheran, blanket and shawl
The chill of winter affects us all.

Exciting is the snow that falls -
Looks like those white cotton balls.
I hear the echo of mother's call
'Take care lest you slip and fall!'

Icicles hang from roofs and walls
This grand sight enthuses, enthrals.
Gather around all naughty boys
To play with Mother Nature's toys.

Unmindful of the ways they tread
Some boys pay a heavy price.
Their noses become raw and red
When they feast on snow and ice!

The rush to the doctor multiplies
Patients air their woes and cries.
I too enjoyed the winter thrills
In gardens, parks, mountains, hills.

A crow in the courtyard caws and pleads:
'A price is demanded by all great deeds.'
My mind gets bogged down in wishes and needs
My words lose meaning and my heart bleeds.
But the chill wind of winter will finally ease
- Not far behind is the warm spring breeze.

The **Kangri** or Firepot – an earthenware bowl containing red-hot charcoals and held in a wicker container, unique to Kashmir. It is held under the **Pheran**, a loose robe worn by both male and female Kashmiris, to keep warm in the bitter Kashmir winters. The Pheran robe falls to the feet of a Hindu and to the knees of a Muslim

Resurrection

I slipped into my eventful past.
The film of events glanced by very fast.
My childhood days and the colourful toys,
Some beautiful faces and the naughty boys,
The heat of the summer and the winter chill
Unfreeze the dreams a-wandering still.

When I look back at myself as a child
Reading a book of Oscar Wilde
With my heaviness and body plum'
The music of the rivulet and beat of the drum,
How, gradually I lost my laughter and joys,
Abandoned my home and all of my toys.

The seasons' changes and the mists of life
Have entangled me in a different strife.
The colour of the face has faded now,
Before my Lord I pray and bow,
I ask Him, please, to tell me how –
All the past moments -
To resurrect them now.

The Long Wait

It was not at all easy to sleep that night
Fears and forebodings filled me with fright
The thought of the coming deprivation was biting
A new phase of life it was irrevocably writing.

The preparations had been long going on
We were just awaiting the arrival of dawn.
After prayers we moved down to the courtyard.
Where my mother would soon see us off.

It was a cold dark misty morning
Densely shrouded in cloudy fog,
The silence occasionally broken
By the bark of some distant dog.

As we set off for the Barramulla bus stop
My mother gave me permission to leave
But allowed just fifteen days separation.
Any more would be too much to grieve.

With a last glance at my home I departed
Without showing I was so broken-hearted
Sister, brothers and father bade farewell,
With what inner commotion I cannot tell.
With hugs, embraces and many tears
Too mindful of the future fears
Thus I Boarded the Jammu bus.

The bus kept increasing the distance from home
Multiplying the minutes until hours were done.
The hours became days, and the months became years.
And thus started the long wait between me and my home.

My children grew up, became teens, then young men,
The elder one, then, a bridegroom.

This event created a new space and a room
The long-cherished hope now began to bloom.

The end of the ordeal eventually drew nigh,
Still some more waiting we suffered and bore,
Till at last the craving to heal my homesickness
Soon found me in London *en route* to Lahore.

In London, I waited, this time, the whole night,
While the moon grinned down at my pitiless plight;
I reflected, in pain, on the vaporised past
How things had so changed, so much, and so fast.

In the morning I left for the airport
Where I arrived with guilt feelings and fears
To present myself in my mother's court
Fifteen days had become fifteen years!

The plane was now touching down,
And my heart was beginning to pound.
With all the music of childhood lore,
Soon the steward opened the door.
Lots of images danced my brain
As my mother stepped out of the plane.

Now once again in my mother's embrace
Tears trickling all down my gleeful face
With such an unprecedented, joyful relief
We put to an end fifteen years of pure grief.

What a great healing, what a blessed godsend!
The long years of waiting had come to an end.

Varamul

Varamul is my place of birth,
Its memories bring me joy and mirth.

Set in charming rolling hills
I recollect my childhood thrills:
It lives now in my pulsing heart
Refreshing every single thought.

Remembering all my sorrows and joys;
The hide-and-seek and the wanton boys.
My father's call and mother's taunt;
The sting of quarrels and my brother's haunt.
The beat of the drums with the rhythmic sound.
The Chowk Bazaar and the college ground,
The Sangri Hill and the Gossain Mound,
All these places dance around,
The new Mohalla and the Tehsil Road,
My heart still carries this heavy load.

Moments vanish and time flies,
The dream swims in the vacant eyes.

Varamul is the Kashmiri name for the town of Barramulla in Kashmir.
The **Sangri Hill** is part of Varamul
The **Gossain Mound** holds a Hindu temple, it is on the fringes of Varamul
The **Chowk Bazaar** is a market square
Mohalla is a residential area

Wular Lake

I boarded off to Watlab top
It was a refreshing, redeeming hop.
Nature's bounties have no price,
Idyllic scenes, enchanting, nice.

Lake's vision dances scene by scene
Wular's waters are emerald green.
Look around with eyes so keen -
Exquisite the tomb of Shukar Din.

Around the lake are willows fine,
Stands straight up, the majestic pine.
Wular houses, doonga and boat,
The trapa, the lemna and lotus float.

Wular carries so many secrets,
Chirp mallards, shovelers, pintails, egrets.
I once went out on a long boat ride,
I was washed ashore by the rising tide.

I have memories of Wular deep inside,
For me, in the lake, many treasures hide.
With its over-abundant vegetation and fish
We could always enjoy a sumptuous dish.

What to Egypt is the Nile River
The same to Kashmir is sweet Wular,
Or, like Siberia's Lake Baikal -
Wular gives blessings to each and all.

Watlab is a hilltop where you can stand and look down upon Wular Lake
Shukar Din is a Kashmiri saint
Doonga is a houseboat
Trapa are nuts. **Lemna** is floating cattle fodder. **Lotus** is water-lily, the root is eaten with fish. They are all water plants
Chirp mallards, shovelers, pintails and **egrets** are Siberian migratory water birds

Festivals

*Human equality is the strain of my song
All sinners and repentants come along*

Nazrul-Islam "The Destitute"

Barbeque
Hairath
Merry Christmas
My Eid Day
My Valentine
On Sighting the Eid Moon

Barbeque

That Saturday morning in an English courtyard,
Away from the maddening world of discord,
That morning when I sat to pray
I planned some moments for the day.

At Upton Park I caught the train,
Strange-eyed constellations irked my brain.
The courtesy of good manners is alive still.
The pleasure of happy folk never grows chill.

Guests with smiling faces arrived for the meal
Their pleasant anticipation, on it put a seal.
The barbeque was arranged in the open ground,
The whiff of lamb chops wafted all around.

During the day we had glorious sunshine,
In the evening we eagerly waited the fun-time.
Some of the guests were seated, the children on the run,
Special entertainment preparations were well done.
(Such occasional obligations we should never, ever shun.)

The barbeque and party had proceeded very well,
It was joy and celebration as everyone could tell.
When the fun was over, and we were left alone,
We had surely done in Rome, as the Romans would have done.

Thus Yasir and his family entered their new home.

My friend, **Yasir**, invited me to his housewarming party

Hairath

The cosmos smiled,
The universe laughed
The galaxies exclaimed with joy,
Announcing the cosmic dance
To celebrate the joyous union
Of a great celestial couple.

Beneath a perfumed sky
With music of peeling bells
They are telling it out
That this event, full of grace,
The heavenly embrace,
Brings Shiva and Parvati
To tie the knot.

In an atmosphere dazzling bright
For a wondrous nuptial night
Known as Shivratri
This cosmic wedlock
Is celebrated to unlock Love
And to bury Hate.

I used to visit my Pandit friends,
Colleagues and belovèd gems
To exchange greetings on this date.
Now they are far away by fate,
And I miss the dishes that I ate.
On this festival of pickled walnuts and fish
I enjoyed many a taste of each sumptuous dish!
Each year I visited my friends at their homes
Bearing gifts of sugar, almonds and cardamoms.
Remembering Hairath took me to those alleys
Where my spirit still roams,
- Where my soul still dallies.

Hairath (meaning 'surprise'), also known as **Shivratri,** is an important festival celebrated by the Kashmiri Pandits

Merry Christmas

Christmas, festival of joy
For every adult, girl and boy;
To children it brings a lot of fun
They merrily gad about and run
Waiting impatiently for Santa's gifts
Away from the sordid world of rifts
Santa carries a variety of treats
Children enjoy his toys and sweets.

Colourful, glistening, Christmas trees!
Children deck them in twos and threes.
Prayers are held in church and home,
With carols, candles, holly, mistletoe,
Bells in the churches constantly ring
While people meditate, pray and sing.

Turkey is the choicest Christmas dish
Other days people enjoy fish and chips!
There are parties, dancing and the ball
The magic of Christmas affects us all.

I too, enjoyed a Christmas night
Every nook and cranny bathed in light
People were smiling, happy and merry
Celebrating Christ's birth anniversary
Sent to this planet to save and unchain
Put balm on our wounds and heal our pain
He frees humanity from Satan's bondage.

Christ is love, light and thunder
He is nature's greatest wonder!
Dispelling anger and conquering rage
He is part of our blessed heritage
He thus belongs to every age.

Merry Christmas and happy New Year!
This message with you I'd like to share.

Written on the 26th December 2008

My Eid Day

Eid is a carnival of joyful moods
It is a festival of cuisines and foods.
The day begins by bowing to the Creator
He is the Merciful, the Great Protector.

All praises be to my Lord
Everything occurs by His word.
This day of joys is very rare
It is celebrated twice a year.

Children have a seldom chance
The whole day they sing and dance,
Little girls have lots of fun
They look brighter than the stars and sun.

On this day in my mind I fly back to my land.
I remember the playgrounds, the earth and the sand
I come across rivers and valleys and streams,
But on their banks humanity screams!

For a moment I forget all of my joy
In the hands of destiny am I a toy?
This very thought winds up my heart
The whole day is spent untying the knot.

Every Eid strengthens my determination,
I will return in dignity to my destination.
On that day I will surely say:
"Today is my Eid Day".

Eid is a festival of sacrifice, of fast-breaking, marking the end of Ramadan, the month of fasting

My Valentine

A spirit caged under an old tortoise shell
Was struggling to free itself to tell
That beauty is God's handwriting
And ugliness, too, is God's will.

I was gingerly turning the page
To read the meaning of this message.

But as this was taking place
I looked up to see a beaming face
Robed in radiant costume
Wafting fragrance of intoxicating perfume.

I marvelled at this wondrous sight
Emanating dazzling light,
A damsel, beautiful and fine
Declared, "I am your valentine!"

On Sighting the Eid Moon

Through the tear in my eye, now the Eid moon
Provokes a sigh through the brownish gloom.
As she peers back at me through clouds wild and dark
She kindles in me that creative spark.

Strange to think, in the dead of night
She eclipses the sun by day so bright
This spurs me on to greater heights
Not to be hindered by new delights.

With the arrival of joys of the festive Eid
The thought of separation makes me heed
- Momentarily to forget all woes,
Kindly to forgive our enemies and foes.

To enrich the blessings of human esteem
The moon appears now as a dazzling dream
Come to assuage my predestined qualms
By the warmth of people with open arms.

Come out and have a look at this moon
Don't miss this moment - come out soon –
Let's fly up there to plant a kiss
On this Eid moon, in our moment of bliss!

Eid is celebrated twice; as a mark of thanksgiving and also celebrated to remember the supreme devotion shown by the Prophet Ismail (AS) to his father Abraham (AS). It is a festival of sacrifice.

Mystery

*Discover yourself; find the key
No blossoms are borne by a withered tree
There is a curtain you cannot see
What is the difference between you and me*

Out of the Depths

A Priceless Thought
An Invitation
Do the Moments Die?
Infinity
Just in Sight
Lost Dream
Self-Speaking
Solitude versus Fortitude
The Unsung Song
Unexpected Expectation
When Shall the Mercy Flow?

A Priceless Thought

Suddenly towards the fake end of night,
When the full moon is about to sink out of sight,
I open my eyes in stark disbelief.
Anticipating some God-given, heaven-sent relief.
Perceiving that somebody is whispering
Politely seeking some answers.

Maybe this is an inaccurate contemplation
Perhaps it is just some mindless speculation.
My fancy is caught at a crossroads in the crossfire;
The ideal is too precious, too strong my desire.
Belief and disbelief are at daggers drawn
As a black mist shrouds the advancing dawn.

Quite distinctly I find myself in the midst of turpitude.
In the whirlwind of loneliness my comfort is my solitude.
I have suppressed many an outspoken shout,
Weathered many a dreary drought.
I fiddle and fondle in a thoughtful wheeze;
Suddenly my feet in motion freeze.

Should I keep my lips tight
At this appalling sight
And wait till it arrives?
Till my priceless thought thrives?

An Invitation

If you come to my home some day
And in my room you stay,
Leave your worries at bay.
Look inwards and pray.

My room has things large and small
Please, observe them one and all.
Books and diaries are on a big shelf
They contain wisdom for power and inner-self.

There are pictures on the table, with frames
Like faded, long-extinguished flames.
There are containers with broken edges and bases,
Dried flowers higgledy-piggledy in vases.

A look at this scattered mess
Sends a shiver down spine and flesh.
The drawers are worth a few rummages,
They're full of yellowed pages and long-lost images faded.

Words are chiselled into the walls.
These peep into my moistened eyeballs.
Rivers of tears in the darkness of the night I shed.
Lack of sleep is evident from the restlessness of my bed.

All this sufficient to express
The seriousness of my great distress.
Someone has to be Jude or Hardy's Tess.

A journey to my home would be a rewarding venture,
If you would like to share my consternation,
Or even, bestow your censure,
Please accept my invitation.

Do the Moments Die?

To conquer loneliness and solitude
I struggle with great fortitude.
The day is spent thus with some ease
But come the night the commotion does increase.

Dark shades are flitting all around,
I just hear a hissing sound.
Memories both good and bad abound,
Of no avail to beat the ground.

I enter then my realm of dreams,
For a while I swim in an ocean of screams
I rail at the pain of self within
I abhor the greed for power and spin.

I open the windows of my mind
Tap right in to the pain of mankind.
My agony thus I multiply,
I discover then we are *all* small fry!

There's a mighty fall into a chasm of night
The darkness provides a satanic sight.
Fears fade for a grand resistance,
Then I forget my own fleeting existence.

From the vast darkness emerges a moon with light
A grand, enthralling, uplifting sight.
I bathe now in the moonlight clear,
I cast off worries, fright and fear.

Then follows a flashback - and again I cry
Do the moments really die?

Infinity

Depths as of unsounded ocean,
Heights as of unconquered mountain.
From scattered shards of a flower vase,
To the magnitudes of a desert vast;
From the forest and the hill and vale
Resounds the writ of Nature's tale
The Artist's perfection.
Nature's reflection
Universal renewal
Change and upheaval
Sun scatters Light
So the day is bright.
The evening's delight
With a moonlit night.
Be it sun
Or
Be it moon,
We discover soon
That the sun is source
For
Wondrous discourse -
To
Emanate rays
To
Brighten the days
Lending its light.
To
The moon for the night.
The celestial dance continuing since ages
Without contempt for monotonous phases
Starting from zero and going to infinity
We grasp the ultimate sovereign Divinity.

Just in Sight

The darkest crevices, here, in my soul
Are searching now for light;
The loved-ones who have slipped away,
Their faces radiant, bright
Have left us all on the freezing bay
Where flames of fury flicker and shine
While a number of devils dance and dine
This aching and stinging is driving me mad,
These frenzied-filled thoughts are making me sad.

These burning desires provoke me to rise
Take up arms and put on a most valiant guise
To cut all the detractors down to size, but…
Such intentions engender disgust and surprise.

Memory lane with its bounties of old
And powerful thoughts that provoke my mood
They bite at my body and strike a chill cold
But provide me with appropriate food.

It sustains me whilst swimming in the ocean of ecstacy
Helping me conquer every swell of fright
Enlivening, augmenting the fearful fantasy
Furthering my goal, which is now, just in sight.

Lost Dream

Self affirmed esteem
Craves the unrealised dream.
Treading along the spiral path
Shrouded in miraged froth
Stumbling, standing, on the run,
Gazing upon the clouded horizon.
Necessity of endless doubts
Prepares me for these many bouts.
While searching for my endless dream
At times I feel I have to scream.
Discovering now, a poisonous demon
Vomiting out unlimited venom.
My search unearths a sensational show
Of humans perpetually beating their brow.
I emerge upon a zigzag road
To unburden myself of my heavy load.
The rust of converging thoughts is encroaching;
Upon my lofty desire it is poaching.
At what cost
The dream is lost.

Self-speaking
- A conversation with myself -

Night is darker than sight,
And breathing - a laborious fight.
The perception of piercing pain is evident,
The shock of loss is predominant.
How to mourn the lost trust?
No hands available for beating the breast.
Every beat of the heart,
Reflects the tragedy in part.

Confidence is shaken in the envisioned future,
A tremor is shaking my brain's every suture.
Like the atheist, who does not believe in God,
Who dares not give the affirmative nod,
How can I arrange a tryst?
On all sides there is fog and mist.
There is a need for resurrection,
Many have lost self-direction.
Ideas have been stolen,
Feelings have been frozen.

The universe is a mystery shrouded in stars,
Although we have conquered the moon and soon mars
We have failed on the earth and also the sand,
On our own slippery soil we still cannot stand.
The agony, pain and the long-lingering slumber,
Cause the wry sluggard to languish and lumber.

Many a brilliant gem in distress,
Has lost its ability or power to express.
It heaves a sigh,
It fails to cry.
In such a summer of helpless misery,
Great self-discovery was found in soliloquy.

Solitude versus Fortitude

Should I continue to write verses in rhyme,
Portraying my conviction and not killing time?
Is there anyone who can read the pain in my tears?
My feelings give meaning to human fears.

We weave the future in dreams
As we are hurt in convulsing screams.
Who can put balm on my wounded heart?
Or pull my frozen lips apart?

Who will read my blurrèd eyes?
Who will count my shocks and sighs?
Doesn't everybody know
Untreated wounds continue to grow?

When we come across beautiful, lifeless eyes,
They pierce the unconscious with deplorable ties.
Who is the promoter?
The aching emoter?

The season of separation and solitude
Requires great patience and fortitude.
Who will tread with me the zigzag path?
Stray far and wide from home and hearth?

No way and no saviour?
No wind, no clouds, no slaver!
Whatever was written in black and white
Has faded in the blinding light.

Loneliness and solitude deepen everyday,
While the sun shines, I can make no hay.
Let us come out of this world of dreams:
Let's *heed* the wretches' cries and screams!

The Unsung Song

A delightful presence
Conquered every form of resistance.
There descended on all sides a thoughtful silence
Arousing much-needed acceptance.
The lips trembled to tell
My greatest find, farewell;
Birds broke out of their shells,
Divinity started ringing the bells
Time just came to a stop
Announcing my life's greatest hop
Authoring new wordage
Heralding a thrilling message.

The soul mate conquers every impediment and block
Although confronted with shock after shock.
As a child's excitement in gifts of toys
New knowledge bounded all my joys.
It was a breezy sting
Autumn transforméd into spring.
A void in a life usually chills;
Every form of happiness thrills.
Exploring all the charms.
The guest was received with open arms.

All this happened in such great haste.
Departure's poison I had to taste;
Silence descended on every song;
The visitor's absence would be long.
Helplessness then knocked at the doors
Thus flowered again all the wounds and sores
Which failed to give meaning to my dreams
But witnessed commotion and parental screams.

Some stories must remain untold.
Relations outweigh silver or gold,

Dreams and destiny we cannot buy,
Unrealised emotions burst and cry.
Gardens in the midst of winter, freeze,
No fragrance, no flowers, no breeze.
A peep at the golden cascade
Revealed a massive silver shade.

Revelation for me is very rare,
I am hesitant to tell my mum –
You help me rub on some balm,
The waiting has been very long,
It's time to sing the unsung song.

Unexpected Expectation

Sometimes one fails to perceive
How one is destined to achieve
A position of greatest pride
When nobody is on one's side.

An unimaginable commotion is born,
Hopes remain but nightmares warn.
Moving ahead with tender care,
The vagaries of nature one has to share,
Warmth as well as the cold to bear.
Watch the front, protect the rear,
Come out of self-deception
Have a realistic perception.
Do not heed a shadow or a picture,
Be mindful of the emotional stricture.
Speak the less and think the more,
That is the lesson one was taught before.

Ideas always unfold
Dreams are never sold.
Voices are calling one to one's destination
One must heed
The unexpected expectation.

When Shall the Mercy Flow?

With all benediction and trust
This is my conscious thrust

To raise a forceful voice
With the prick of conscience
And by choice

For all those who suffer the pain
In bus, at home, on tube, in train
For all acts of ignominious distain

By those so ignorant
Of the ever-binding human chain.

Wherever my eyes view
Scenes which are so very true
Scattered limbs and body parts
The heart wriggles and starts
For the unfulfilled
The scattered dreams, dashed.
I utter cries and screams
For each and every body smashed

When shall all the perpetrators bend?
When shall all the torments end?
When shall all the faces glow?
When shall the mercy flow?

Love

*But love will always find a way
to still the sweet desire*

Fazal Shah "Sohni Mahewal"

Award
Eternal Love
Flashback
Morning Breeze
Peace
The Conquest
Unfinished Task

Award

I 've kept on knocking at your door
I have convulsed upon your floor
Been consumed with many wishes
Wasted some delightful dishes!
Missed spring's most refreshing breeze,
Eaten humble pie with ease.

Pangs of hunger, pain and gloom
In my heart and eager eyes bloom.
Although the moments will ultimately wane
It's a tragic story down the drain.

I still adore you
And implore you.
No sticks nor stones
Shall break my bones.

Do not kick me in your thought -
You are the one whom I have sought.
Come and grace me with your charm
You won't come to any harm.

Your presence would be fair reward.
The time has come for this award.

Eternal Love

The tragedy of a brimming life begins
When in spite of all the follies and the sins,
In spite of knowing all details
Our ego dominates and our friendship fails
And we shroud our life in dens and veils.

A deep emotion the individual feels.
Time flies by and the heart is sealed.
Expressions falter, the tongue is stilled.
The wrong is not righted.
The friend is not sighted.

No word of affirmation dawns.
The broken heart in sunset yawns.
No message flashed
All hopes are dashed.

A new feeling silently grows
The passion deepens as it shows
The sign of a great commotion,
Displaying profound emotion,
The song of the flying dove –
The call of eternal love.

Flashback

Midsummer madness carried me away
Escaping the crowd to a farmhouse for rest, sleep and solitude.
Soon on a couch I lay and fell deeply asleep.
What I saw is worthy of narration:

Some supernatural force tossed me in the sky,
Placed me on a large cloud to fly,
Energised by my imagination.
To a world of fascination.

Floating over mountains, meadows and streams,
Landing me finally in the garden of my dreams –
My *alma mater*, my temple of learning,
My unforgettable college.

Greeted by the fragrance of flowers with their jostling heads
Their myriad colours connecting long-lost threads.
Thus I entered the decorated hall
A place that is imprinted indelibly upon my life.

With its unforgettable and precious moments
Which have become eternal;
It was here I frolicked with a radiant damsel
A paragon of beauty whose golden hair I fondled.
I share these words uttered in ecstasy –

With you.

They are ever ringing
And nymphs are ever singing
Whenever I think of her blessed existence,
My feelings crave for some token expression.

And to conquer the distance across God's creation
I commune with my Lord and implore him to give just a nod,

To preserve her from strife
To grant her a life
That is glorious…
Of a sudden, roused from my dreamtime intimations
I'm again back on track.

It was just a flashback.

Morning Breeze

In spring our hearts dance with desire of love.
The rose of life its fragrance thus enhanced,
Enhances Love.
Love glows in our eyes-
Eyes, which sometimes love their tears,
Our lips whisper softly through the cries.
Butterflies are flitting free of fears.

Love is a delicate water bubble
The only remedy for all my trouble.
It reflects in the beauty of a moonlit night
It pierces through every beautiful sight.
It speaks to us through the twinkling stars
It reverberates through the rhythmic strumming
Of guitars.
It is a truthful dedication
Leading to a spiritual emancipation.

Love is the life beating in our hearts
Love is a cherub shooting us with his darts.
Love is a lullaby lulling us in our thoughts.
Love is in the child's smile
Recharging the spirit of its mother awhile.

Sometimes when old memories tease
Love creeps in like the morning breeze.

Peace

Peace, the abode of love
Peace, the journey of a flying dove
Peace, an envoy of Paradise
Peace, the people's unified voice.

Peace, a soothing ray of light
Peace, a flame so bright
Peace, a perpetual solace
Peace is God's beautiful grace.

Peace is my universe's beautiful face
Peace is humanity's case
Peace distances us from hate
Peace is my heart's wondrous gate.

Peace rouses your conscience
Peace conquers your hateful intransigence
Peace stabilises your stances
Peace eliminates cruel nuances.

Peace irrigates the sands of deserts
Peace evolves principles for your comforts
Peace is pitted against oppression
Peace cures all your deep depression.

Peace does not have a border line.
Peace is needed all the time.

The Conquest

Shadows of a long evening of pain
Tempt me, tellingly, yet again,
To sing my song, my sad refrain.

Let us peep, deep into this seething heart
With a polished lens and a pencilled chart.
Trading Pain, for Love, in the bitterest cold
Well aware that the glitter is not real gold.

Awaiting the arrival of my esteemed Guest
With my best suit on, in my zeal and zest.

The destined stranger will knock at my door
To pour precious balm on my troubles sore.
All my apprehensions will be laid to rest
And I am sure, by this means, I will pass the test.

The sweet smell of success will spread in the vale,
All around will be echoed this joyful tale.
That Love can conquer, is easily taught.
It can purify every human thought.

Unfinished Task

Let us create for ourselves a heritage,
Free from the convulsions of hate of our age.
A world full of vibrant colours
A world full of fragrant flowers
Creating space
Giving a place
For the threatened butterfly,
To thrive and to multiply
To strengthen our loving tie.

In this commitment let me, myself, immerse,
To succour, to comfort and to nurse -
My dream, embedded in this, my verse.
Perceiving the perils to be eschewed,
Finding the fire of hope renewed.

The flame of love we must ignite
'Gainst demons of hatred we should fight.
Tolerance and decency must be our creed.

Let us sow this precious seed.
In the light of accomplishment let us all bask -
If we complete, together, this unfinished task.

Illusion

The gardens bloom and the flowers yearn
To tell the gardener, don't grumble just learn
Colours fade, beauty vanishes turn by turn
Unhitch the chains; this secret you'll learn

Reminiscences

A Father's Apology
Death of Dal Lake
Ecstasy
Immortal
Journey to the Unconscious
Paradise Turned into Hell
Repeat, Repeat
The Flower Vale Cries Out for Spring
The Land of Gloom

A Father's Apology

My child, my insensitivity you'll forgive.
I know the conditions in which you live.
Everyday the news I read and view.
I learn of the agonies faced by you.
Death and destruction is the order of the day;
Everybody lacks the courage to say
'Stop this murder, revenge and insanity!
Be in harmony with the call of humanity.'
I know what is what and who is who
But nothing can I do.

My eyes observing such a sight,
My conscience wriggles with a fright.
Innocents consigned to flame and fire,
An old woman's safety is dear and dire.
I can hear my mother's doleful cries
I cannot see her tearful eyes;
In the lap of his father, a child dies.
My eye, it weeps; my heart it bleeds;
The writing on my wall, it reads:
"*You know what is what and who is who,*
– But nothing can you do!"

My child, my insensitivity you'll forgive.
I know the conditions in which you live.
I am busy with in-fighting everywhere,
Your enemy, alas, I cannot disappear.
I have my own problems and wars.
On my body I carry the ethnic scars.
My latter-day politics causes others to fight.
Of caste and region I am flying the kite!
Opposition to unity is a shameful spite.
Poverty and disease make for dreadful plight,
Most of my brethren neither read nor write.
On every side I am ensnared;

To the rising tide my chest is bared,
My soul, every day this sad fact shares.
I know what is what and who is who
But nothing can I do.

My child, not my own intuition alone
Tells me your war of attrition is won -
Not bullet, nor rocket nor, even, the bomb
Will ever consign your creed to the tomb.
Victory is your destiny and this is known!
You will shake off the oppressor, see!
You do not need the likes of me,
Chained by hate and acrimony.
I know what is what and who is who
But nothing can I do.

Afraid they are, the powers that be,
Eyes they have and they can see –
This is confirmed in history.
They know it all too well;
The future they can surely tell –
Ultimately you will leave behind
These dreadful, harrowing, fearful times
And bring to an end these heinous crimes.

You know what is what and who is who
That your persistence will win through!

Death of Dal Lake

Viewed from the garden of Parimahal
Eyes are soothed by the sprawling Dal.
At a distance stands Makhdoom's shrine -
A magnificent edifice, ancient, sublime.

The Dal and the Nigin here, both merge,
Inviting a pensive, alluring urge.
In dazzling colours the shikaras small
Are placed on the banks for one and all.
Nigin's waters of emerald green
Sparkle and flash with diamantine sheen.
Watching the gardens floating by
Is the grandest sight for the inward eye.
When you've done listening to nature's sitar
Board the boat to Char Chinar.

Far away from my Srinagar, I am crying,
Saddened to know, with the time that is flying,
Neglect, encroachment, garbage lying,
Waters receding, the Dal is dying.

Dal Lake is one of the many famous lakes in Srinagar
Parimahal is the Mughul observatory from the time of King Shah Jahan
Makhdoom is the Sufi saint, Sheikh Hamza
Nigin is a Kashmiri lake near the Dal
Char Chinar is a small natural island in Dal Lake which has four Chinar trees, one on each corner of the island

Ecstasy

It is always a distant destination
Reflecting on an appalling situation.
I get absorbed in my own imagination
Endemic is poverty and acute starvation
With all this unpleasant load of misery
I feel I fail at my chivalry
I forget my youth in its prime.
I look busy all the time.

There are some moments full of concern
When my deepest emotions truly burn
I get drowned in memories of old
For a few moments they make me bold.
I remember the face and the golden cascade,
The brow and the eyes of a radiant comrade.

The air is filled with exotic perfume
My friend arrives in his paragon costume.
Dances my heart with a warming glow
Forgotten my cares and my feelings of woe.
I forget all my qualms, the depressing distress.
I become free of sorrow, wonderfully blest
A thrill engulfs me in perfect ecstasy.

Then somebody taunts me, dispelling my fantasy.

Immortal

Immortal hands designed my stage
Do not disregard this historic page.
My heart is aching, my soul is hurt.
Gems of wisdom are sullied in dirt.

The gardens have lost their beauty and charm,
The flowers have been damaged and come to harm.
The night and the Shalimar were always my haunting,
But the state of the garden is woefully daunting.

The soul of man has abandoned its paradise,
Its departure demands a profound sacrifice.
My lines are expressing this misery and pain,
My mind is confessing its agony again.

Shalimar is a Royal Mughal garden found along the banks of the Dal Lake

Journey to the Unconscious

Touching the thirst of unconscious thoughts
Quenched by those pleasant, undiluted draughts.
The conscious being is in a world of fear
No distance exists 'twixt smile and tear.

The unimagined reality is naked and nude
Deep questions flirt in such solitude.

The human body in bones encaged
The purpose of existence to be gauged
Looking inwards questions the soul
- What, after all, is to be the goal?

Resting the heart and exerting the brain
Discovering deep down, the meaning of pain,
Doubting one's being and starting with doubt,
Exerting the mind makes ready the bout.

In questioning the thinking mode
Set your face firm and trudge this road
Go not astray but keep moving on
Personal virtues will tune your song.

The world today is in a state of rout
Disregard all the thorns and do not shout.
No one else will right those wrongs
Choose, instead, your own beats and songs.

A journey to the unconscious will make you bold,
Will warm conscious thought and numb the cold.

Paradise Turned into Hell

As through Paradise I made my way
Fairies and angels stayed at bay.
The sky was bathed in the light of stars
I stood swinging between moon and mars.

No milk flowed in brooks or streams
Martyrs' souls wandered by in teams.
The nightingales were in a state of mourning
The gardener too was crying and bawling -
'Evil has entered paradise!
The dwellers have lost their laws.
What can be the cause?'

I raised the question and asked to know
Who was behind this murderous show.
In thoughtlessness I wondered.
My soul was severely plundered.
Gradually revealed to me through the mirror
The tale of the crimes and the cause of the terror –

Indian thugs on a killing spell.
Paradise converted into Hell!

Repeat, Repeat!

Ah! Memories delightfully sweet
Recalling them is a wondrous treat
Throbbing with every new heart-beat
Calling me again to repeat, repeat!

On a hillside; a grassy mound,
This is where I played around
Here, reminiscences abound.
Where my mind's eye kisses the ground!

Was it 'Beauty and the Beast'?
Convivial friends and a sumptuous feast
The loud, the carefree, wanton cries
The wide, alluring, sparkling eyes!

What a world of tremendous fun!
We were all gadding, on the run,
By the moon at night, or in the sun
We all agreed, 'twas jolly well done!

Such treasured moments, sadly,
Flit in, then out, of mind
But keep on repeating, gladly,
From time to time.

The Flower Vale Cries Out for Spring

Give me answers, I implore!
Forgive me for exposing a festering sore.
But my soul is in search of answers
From city magicians, carpenters and barber;
From all the professional engineers
Who construct lifeless, unwanted structures.

The city dwellers have been told
Deploy men and women, many fold.
Look after the much-loved fort;
Consider it a duty, not a sport.
See the morning sun,
Label it the evening moon, don't shun.

May I ask a question
Of the grand city magician
And the master dyer, the politician
Of the self-trumpeted theoretician?
One who abandoned his cherished convictions?
His forehead is in a state of turmoil.
He has disgraced all the sons of the soil.

Why has our Babel so many conflicting powers?
Who fashioned these blossoms with paper flowers?
A labour of love, or a juggler's trick?
Or just another paper stick?
The blood of martyrs calls for an inward look.
Do not ignore it. Read that book.

Permit me to ask the question.
Pardon me for enquiring
Why Nishat has lost enchantment and wonder
Why all the great desires have gone asunder
And why Shalimar is shrouded in autumn mist,
And the waters of the Dal have all gone amiss.

The thirsty Wular disturbs my mind
The Lidar of Pahalgam has gone blind.
The birds have heard bang after bang,
The nightingale has lost its sang.
Prem Nath is in such painful plight
Karnail yearns for a beautiful sight.

Mehmood makes no choice.
Hassan Sofi's lost his melodious voice,
The Ghazal of Rasul Mir's lost its rhyme
The criminal's free to commit his crime.

O gardener see Mahjoor's flower vale,
My people now, will brook no sale!

The **Wular** is Asia's largest fresh water lake
The **Lidar** is a small river in Kashmir on which stands the Pahalgam health resort
Prem Nath symbolises the Kashmiri Pandits
Karnail symbolises the Kashmiri Sikhs
Mehmood is the Kashmiri poet Mehmood Gami
Hassan Sofi is a well-known Kashmiri singer
The Ghazal of Razul Mir is a collection of rhythmic verses in Kashmiri/Urdu
Mahjoor is a Kashmiri national poet

The Land of Gloom

The rosary of dear friends,
The shining, the reciting gems,
Whenever these diamonds come to life in my eyes
The environs get saddened with my moans and sighs.

The bygone colours become blurred.
The long-lost interests get rekindled.
Tears trickle down my whiskers
With the memory of that lost paradise.

My skin creeps and tingles.
In these moments of pain;
In such atmosphere of agony and disdain
I become pensive in vain - and sickened.

This slap of conscience feels so bad.
I start hearing straight from the heart
The sordid tales of friends past.
I become quite impatient and sad.

I am not eager to share, hand-in-glove
With friends who care,
When those near and dear - who broke the bond of love,
- Slipped into the unknown,
- Said goodbye to the world that is known,
On the other side of the horizon to dally
In a still, calm valley,
In a world of forgetfulness -
Drowning forever in darkness spreading all about.

A sudden caricature of all that is lost bites the heart
To shout - numbing the blood-drenched echoes,
Convulsing in eternal wails and woes.

Humanity

Glow-worms light up their nights
And crickets sing lullabies affectionately
It is the breath of purest love
Restores the dead to life

Jasim-ud-Din "The Grapes"

A Tribute to Londoners
Dreams Cannot be Sold
Echoes of Palestine
God's Handwriting
Long Live Humanity
The Rest of the Windows are Shut
Will You Be my Friend?

A Tribute to Londoners

We all owe a debt,
My eyes are wet,
As I cry and say,
The 7th of July was a doomsday.
Londoners have braved their way,
Their glory will remain and stay,
Their courage will reward and pay,
Tormentors will be kept at bay.
There is no fear.
There is no fright.
The sun is shining ever bright,
With the help of other people's might,
We will protect our every right.
Londoners have put all at stake,
Terror-mongers will finally break,
The world-conscience we will shake,
For a grander future's sake.
Let us not cry or shriek,
Let us rise up and speak,
Terror has risen to its peak.
Everybody's help we seek:
The Imam and the Panditji,
The Priest and the Rabbi,
To sit together at a wisdom feast,
To defeat the ugly terrorist beast.
Let peace be
The clarion call,
For every country large or small,
To protect every citizen's life,
To end the feuding and the strife.
We are all human, after all.
Be they old,
Be they teens,
All are simply human beings;
We are passing through a testing time,

We are witnessing a gruesome crime,
We only have one simple choice;
To condemn it with one single voice.
That day will definitely dawn,
When we will surely sit and fawn,
On the banks of the ocean of love,
Overlooked by the flying dove.

Remembering the victims of the 7th July 2005 terrorist attack in London

Dreams Cannot be Sold

There is no reason for cheering in a motionless ocean;
Deep within me is burning an incessant fire,
The darkness of the night seems a calming potion.
But self-esteem, my prized possession, is very, very rare.

My distances are stranded by a collective pain,
My friendships all are hinged in a common human chain.
The slumbering legends are coming now to life;
The awakening charms are melting away the strife.

The day of reckoning is nearly just at hand
When my caricatures will dance
To the tunes of a big brass band.

The sayings of the wise are very, very old:
Dreams can never, ever be sold.

Echoes of Palestine

The land of the Prophets is in great turmoil,
Blood spills profusely on Palestine's soil;
Wherever you look, all around the blood flows;
With each passing moment, the tension still grows.
The blood of its people has become very cheap,
The wide gaping wounds are now very deep.
Be it blood of a Muslim, Christian or Jew -
It is not to be seen as a mere drop of dew.

Sharon is a modern invincible czar;
But he will soon fall like a shooting star,
Humanity, till then, slumbers on, deep;
Harvest of corpses ... who will it reap?
Alas! We are left with only one course:

To improve every single available resource,
To triumph over the assailant's temerity.
Not to lose heart; not to lose hope;
Your future, my friends, has truly great scope:
For the day's not far off when you will create
A free, independent Palestinian State!

God's Handwriting

With the arrival of Eve
Arrived womanhood,
With her power of unlimited love
With her propensity to resist.
And unfathomable combination
Of virtues and vices
The tenderness and the delicacy
The divine morphology.
Bouts of good and evil
The secret melody
The eternal ecstasy.

Poets make her their subject,
And artists depict her contours,
Converting her into an immortal Mona Lisa.
Whilst history is recording her every achievement
And kings quarrel over the right to her passions
And advertisers are selling us her smiles.
Placing her on the highest of pedestals
Which can be seen for miles

But her march for liberation continues,
Challenging hollow civilisation's
Fickle foundations.
Breaking all ties
With those obsolete norms.
Although some narrow minds
Still block her path
Inviting her wrath
Yet her march
Still continues
Facing the storms.

And this fact informs us
That whilst the path-blockers,

Confined in a shell,
Continue to propagate
False precepts from Hell,
Nevertheless, Eve, still continues to swim
Without fear or fancy or whim.

So, let us relinquish
Our staid hibernation.
Be part of her journey,
Provide her with every
Sincere facilitation
For her swift and sure,
Full, and final liberation.
Abandon the much-staked back-biting.
After all,
She is God's own handwriting.

Long live Humanity

People all over the world,
Join the people of America to say
The 11th of September was a doomsday.
Appointment with terror straight from the sky,
The dead feel no pain. They utter no cry.
It was an act insane,
Such
Agony and pain.
All were caught unawares,
The assailants dropped into the Pentagon,
And the International Centre for Trade,
There was a panic obscene, terror all round,
The hundred ten stories twin towers –
All razed
To the ground.
By the time this news broke,
It was all up in smoke.
The sun was still shining ever so bright,
Yet day was tipped into darkest night.
When I reflect on events of this kind
My tenderness of heart and mind,
Makes me say
Humanity in peril
Has to lick these wounds,
Till we come out of our shell,
And in the light of patience,
Get over this hell,
Have respect for all,
End every strife,
And understand
The true value of life.
The blood of humans is all the same,
Those who shed it,
Incur but shame.
All the great religions teach,

To respect the dignity of man.
And preach
Tolerance, good will and love to each,
We must do what we can.

A decision should never be taken in haste;
Haste will always make more waste.
Conquer the minds and hearts of foes
By the twin towers of tolerance and love
For the soothing of woes.

A grand reconciliation must take place,
To end conspiracies and plots so base.
We must cautiously step over
The ridges and canyons;
By bridging the gaps and making companions
Of Shakespeare's Shylock,
And all of his minions.

Stop all dry-talk.
From Srinagar to Macedonia,
From Washington to New York,
From Kabul to Jerusalem,
All must strive anew for hope.
Wash the hands that in blood do soak,

Salute the dead,
Move ahead,

For a world of peace without profanity
Declare with me in utmost sanity
Sacred, the Life, of all humanity!

This poem was written in the aftermath of the 9/11 attacks whilst in a hotel in Tehran, and has since been published in various parts of the world

The Rest of the Windows are Shut

How high will you fly?
How hard will you try?
The challenging skies are far above.
Oh men of courage crack the hard nut,
The rest of the windows are shut.

Will you employ all your power?
Reach up through the torrential shower?
When storm clouds on all sides do lour?
How many lighted lamps
Will save you from the stormy clamps?
Keep moving! Keep moving out of the rut.
The rest of the windows are shut.

The restrictions with fuming and fretting,
The stagnation that's already set in,
The hunger, the cursing - the shot!
The rest of the windows are shut.

Way up in space amongst all the stars
We danced on the Moon then soon upon Mars.
Tied to a remote control
How oft will we tumble and roll?
There are still lots of 'ifs" and 'nots' – but
The rest of the windows are shut.

If all of mankind would unite and be one
Harmony in diversity could become
A priceless seed.
A precious creed!
My pain is a visible cut.
The rest of the windows are shut.

Will You Be My Friend?

All the bitterness of the past
All the precious aspirations lost
Exhort my heart,
Exhort my mind,
To make a fresh start.
I offer friendship; take my hand
Bury the hatchet and join my band.
Bid farewell to acrimony and desperation
Demolish 'Berlin walls'- let's end the separation.

Let us say together -
(For the good of each other)-
'Live and let live', the golden rule.
And let this be our future tool.
Come out of the cobwebs and be bold.
We both are fashioned in human mould
By shade of evening and by morning sun
Let's share together life's moments of fun.

Having the same folk-lore
Our rituals and relations match –
Shared vision will lead us to the shore,
There is every reason to mend and patch.

From the day I came here
Your separation I had to bear,
And I'm searching with hope in my eyes
No matter if it eventually dies,
I feel I belong to nobody but you,
Do you share this feeling, too?

Do come to my abode one day
Say anything you'd like to say
I will be no stumbling block.
Denizens, whoever they are,

Are yearning - have a strong desire
To suspend the terror - the frightening fire.

Well-wishers, all, expect us to be sane,
So climb aboard the friendship train.
With honour will you bend?
Won't you be a friend?

Message

There'll be a tremor and each thing will end
Nature herself will set the trend
The stars will fall with a bang and rend
Read this message to all and send

My Country

A Perfect Dawn
Echoes of Kashmir
My Birthright
My Destiny
October the 8th
Questions
Salvation
Simmering Disaster
The Phoenix of Kashmir

A Perfect Dawn

Open your eyes!
Don't be blind,
Clear the blockage from your mind
And look beyond your self-construct.
Do not permit impediment;
Remove the mud and sediment.

Demolish the walls of your hard notions;
Do not writhe in selfish commotions.
There will surely come the time
When you will enter their hearts and mind
With powerful words and thoughts sublime.
It will be the voyage of a sage.
To heal the damage of your age.
Can you perceive the distant glow?
And feel the pulse where cold winds blow?
Telling us something we're trying to know,
Like, which way we really should *not* go?

All it needs is an iron will
To confront the nauseating chill,
Assessing efforts of the past
When the dice were vainly cast.
Voices of reason we have to find
For planning the future of mankind.

We must put a stop to the traders of hate;
With our own bare hands we will write our fate.
With the monster of hatred finally gone
We will welcome, at last, a perfect dawn.

Echoes of Kashmir

Nostalgia and my imagination
Took me off to my destination,
The land of my birth,
My motherland;
A land bearing bruises and scars,
By both, sunlight and shade of stars.
Crying out for justice without discrimination,
Demanding the right of self-determination.
Do not deny us the right to our choice.
Do not suppress this rightful voice.
Be it winter or summer,
Keepers of the world conscience
Let's all not slumber!
Awake! Awake!
The future of a nation is at stake.
The blood-spilling, Kashmir calls you to tame,
Indian thugs are acting without shame.
The people of Kashmir are terrorized,
Men, women and children are brutalized.
This rapacious oppression is perpetrated with rage,
The people of Kashmir are imprisoned in a cage.

Kashmiris, too - are human,
Humans without rights,
In a land of idyllic beauty
And excellent delights.
What this land has come to,
Rends my heart in two.
Each thought shrouded in a tear,
Kashmir is crying in each ear
A part of my nightmare when I sigh.
Nobody living can refute
Jammu and Kashmir in dispute.
The genie of the atom bomb
To be bottled only in a tomb?

Eliminate nuclear confrontation,
Please, end Kashmir's subjugation.
End the trauma of writhing humanity,
Bring peace and its prize of sweetest tranquillity.

Please, see that the morn be soonest to dawn,
When we shall all see,
Occupation over,
And Kashmir free!

My Birthright

Morning breeze
Hit me, to tease.
The soft touch,
This pure air,
Aroused me
Something rare.

Gave life to my dreams
The musical streams.
Became free of strife
Got a new lease of life.

Night descended
Birth of the moon
Started gazing
At me soon
Drowned in waves
The moonlight
Intoxicating
Pure delight.

Forgot every pain
Broke every chain.
Unhitched all my strings
Gave wheels to my wings.

When, suddenly a tsunami of emotions was unfurled,
For me it was a completely different world.
Hypocrisy, double standards and the lies
Carried me away from my murmurings and sighs:

I swim with an over-burdened lot
To scupper and defeat every scheming plot.
I stand again firm, on my own home ground;
And can hear again, still, that melodious sound!

People await, anxiously, my return -
Want to meet and greet me, turn by turn.
Voracious creatures will meet their end.
All the usurpers will have to bend,
Call off their greedy fight
And concede to me my birthright!

My Destiny

Enlivening Nishat, Dal and Shalimar's night
The pathways bathed in soft reflected light;
My unconscious is brimming with all idyllic sights
The parted charms appear in these imaginary flights.
My valued memories come to life.
I unburden my sad, solitary strife.

From unconscious I travel to the conscious state
To uncover the real story of my fate,
When I view this reality show
Let me tell you what I know.

Everywhere continues Satan's dance
No one can stand and take a bold stance
Every word uttered, and every thought bleeds
Who has sown these thorny seeds?
The *iconosphere* wears mysterious halos
As saintly souls kiss the gallows
Their painful cries reverberate
Their shattered hopes hibernate.

In spite of this chill, and deathly cold
We firmly believe and sincerely hold:
Tennyson's words let me remind –
'If winter comes can spring be far behind?'

Awaiting the fulfilment of a brighter dawn,
For all fellow travellers of Life's caravan
Dreams are much more than silver or gold
And, sadly, they can never be sold.
But with courage and determination
We can pledge the affirmation
With wisdom and foresight
We can summon all our might!
Delve deep into my earnest testimony;
With our own hands write our destiny.

Nishat and **Shalimar** are royal Mughal gardens situated on the banks of the Dal Lake
The 'iconosphere' – is that part of the heavens inhabited by the souls of saints and martyrs who are icons on earth
The poem is a tribute to Maqbool Butt who was hanged in Tihar Jail in Delhi on 11th February 1984

October 8th - Disaster in South Asia

Mindful of the fear of Fate,
Death comes to all ere soon or late.
Nature's terror, fury and fright,
Darkness absorbed every ray of light.
Struck the ears a terrible sound,
The Angel of Death danced around.

From rubble the lucky ones were found,
Survivors assembled in open ground.
Many a person still in bed,
Momentarily shrieked and bled,
In large numbers they now lay dead,
Those who saw it thumped their head.
Forty-five seconds were nature's alarm,
The earthquake wiped out every charm,
Devastation for one and all.
Destruction and death hung in a pall.

Far away from this agony and pain,
I am tied by a lasting human chain,
March right in with cash and kind,
The countless victims bear in mind.
Life is cheapened with great disdain,
Survivors are threatened by snow and rain.
Deserving sufferers you have to find,
You have to wonder, search your mind.

One has to ponder, deep and long
Mindful of the fear of Fate,
Death comes to all ere soon or late.

This poem is a commentary on the earthquake which struck in 2005, devastating Kashmir, parts of Pakistan and India

Questions
(Concerning devastation due to earthquakes and war)

The dream, the scene and mild weather;
Where is man's power and high endeavour?
A morning ray
Craves to say
Enjoy the rainbow,
A colourful show.

A silvery sky
Tells you why:
Evolve and grow.
Try to know.

What is the secret of the black night?
An awe-full sight.
Full of stars
Like tiny scars.
The milky way
A glistening tray.

Persistent drought
During the day
Rises to shout:
Where has all the greenness gone –
This crown?

Who wiped it out
From my town
This prize?
Who was it?
Who can it be?
Could it ever have been me?

Salvation

The unfathomable loneliness and the moonlit night
Hammers at my existence in such a plight.
O friend, do you think about all the vicissitudes of life?
Do you have to forge a path through all the strife?
Do you remember me momentarily in the darkening night?
For my part, shunning the flying of an imaginary kite?

The silence speaks and arrows strike my mind,
To do with your unmatchable intransigence.
Time does not wait; it moves with a speed of its own,
Controlling even the cycles of sun and moon.

Make this unbearable separation,
This point of desperation
A Himalayan inspiration.
The partitions of pain
Have to fall.
The fears of time appertain,
Let these continue to crawl.

The only way to overcome such anguish
Is through your own grim determination.

Choose Good,
Not only for your own Salvation!

Simmering Disaster

What consolation in being destiny's child?
Is there no remedy or solution that would fit?
Every sound instinct is ensnared in a whirlwind.
Unbounded and endless is the wilderness of my dreams.

My love, unfathomable, ocean-deep,
Who will pocket it?

Who will retrace for me the path of the dove that has flown?
The morning breeze with me is waiting till you arrive.
Let the moment soon dawn when sweetest thoughts shall thrive.

Oh, Saqi, pour that drop of wine into the cup in my hand,
To sweeten my poisons so that I can withstand
The pain of separation – a simmering disaster -
It will see me through till I become my own master.

The name **Saqi** or 'cupbearer', is often used as a poetic symbol in Urdu depicting a beautiful woman

The Phoenix of Kashmir

Idyllic land of beauty rare, my motherland,
The inspiration of poets, the writer's heaven;
Her glorious parks once again flood into my mind,
Into my heightened consciousness.

Those wonderful scenes of mighty mountains
That change with the shifting light.
The bracing air so fresh and free!
I see again those limpid lakes, fed by her tinkling streams
Which from sparkling springs do flow with melodies sublime,
Her wondrous stately trees in lush forests, majestic, serene,
That march up along her steep hill slopes and climb
Under a radiant sun to meet the bluest sky!

Yet round her peaks and down her valleys bare
Wild storms do lash and maim
In autumnal fury's blinding rage,
Inflicting bruises, damage, daily pain.
At the criminal's behest, their prey, her people,
Do lie in bondage low, struggling in misery,
Dying to escape the captor's blow.

Mythological bird of beauty rare
My motherland, Kashmir!
This vision coming to consciousness
Causes my heart to bleed with drips of blood
That seep, with tears already shed in floods
Into parched and timeless desert sands below.
My words weep silent drops like rain
Mingling there,

To fertilize and nourish the dust of dead folk.

And I believe in the power of Kashmir,
Of her people, whose seeds sown in these, her death throes,

Will take root in these hot ashes, once cooled, and grow again,
Free, at last, from the despot's hand
Free to sing their song of freedom,
Proclaiming the destined course awaiting them,
To rewrite their destiny;
Free, on their own home soil to stand,
So rise again, Kashmir, my motherland!

Accomplishment

> I see images of the loveliest and best
> In silence they forever lie at rest
> Descends a mystical cover on their nest
> Word has it they have passed the test